Nº7 GRANGE &
TIDEWAY STN
MATCHLESS FOR THE

G.SMITH
Dispensing Chemist
WRIGHT'S

# LIVE LIKE A VICTORIAN

## DISCOVERING THE SECRETS OF THE VICTORIANS

CLAIRE SAUNDERS

ILLUSTRATED BY

WESLEY ROBINS

Button Books

# CONTENTS

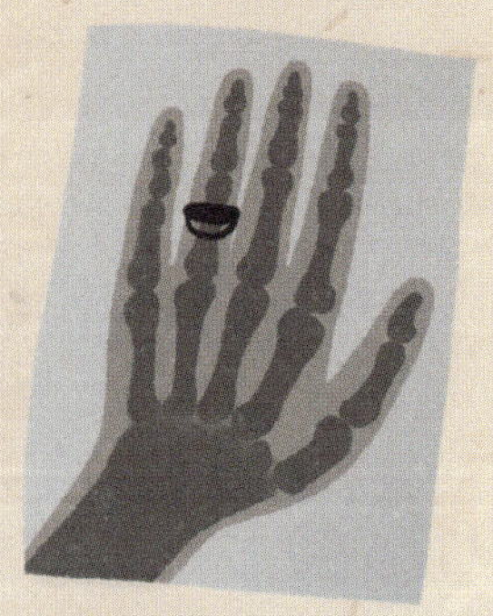

# WHO WERE THE VICTORIANS?

Queen Victoria came to the throne in 1837, and ruled the United Kingdom of Great Britain and Ireland until her death in 1901. This time is known as the Victorian Age. Britain changed a huge amount in these 63 years, as new technology, inventions and ideas transformed the way people lived and worked.

## Industrial might

The Industrial Revolution began during the previous century but gathered speed in the Victorian Age. More people began to live in towns and work in factories. New steam railways and steamships made travel quicker and cheaper for people and for goods. Britain quickly became the world's leading industrial nation. Its empire grew large and powerful too, as British people traded and settled around the world.

## Meet two Victorian children

My name is Will and I'm 11 years old. Six days a week I work in a textile mill, and most days I go to school for a few hours too. Life isn't easy, but there are lots of kids worse off than me. Come with me, and find out about life in a factory town in the 1850s (see pages 16–17). You can see where I live and work, and join me on a day-trip to the Great Exhibition in London (see pages 46–47).

My name is Dora. I am 9 years old and I live in London. My father works as a banker, and my mother looks after the family home. Let me show you what life is like for me in the 1870s. You can find out what I do with my governess all day, what I eat, and what I like to do for fun (see pages 24–25). My family are taking a trip to the seaside soon – you can come too if you like (see pages 38–39).

## Queen Victoria

**Victoria was only 18 when she became queen. Three years later, she married a German prince called Albert. The couple were devoted to each other, and to their nine children. When Albert died aged 42, Victoria was so heartbroken that for the rest of her life she wore nothing but black – the colour of mourning. Over her reign, Victoria became a symbol of British greatness to her people.**

## Everyday lives

In many ways, the Victorian Age was an exciting time. There were big advances in science and medicine. Public libraries, art galleries and museums were built, and great works of literature were written. New inventions like the telephone, electric lighting and sewing machines changed the way people lived.

Yet society was very unequal, and life was desperately hard for lots of people. Many worked in terrible conditions, lived in overcrowded houses and were always hungry. For most people, things did improve by the end of the Victorian Age, but poverty and suffering did not disappear completely.

# TIMELINE OF THE VICTORIAN AGE

These are some of the main events and changes that took place during Victoria's 63-year reign. During this time, the United Kingdom was made up of England, Scotland, Wales and Ireland. Later, in the 1920s, most of Ireland gained its independence and became a separate country, whereas Northern Ireland remained part of the UK.

**1837**
Victoria is crowned queen.

**1840**
The Penny Post is introduced, allowing people to send letters cheaply across Britain for the first time.

**1848**
The first-ever Public Health Act sets up a Board of Health to improve sanitation in towns.

**1838**
The London and Birmingham Railway opens, becoming the world's first long-distance railway line. The same year, the *Great Western* makes its maiden voyage; it's the first steamship built for crossing the Atlantic Ocean.

**1845–9**
Over a million Irish people die in the Great Famine, after the potato crop fails. Many Irish people emigrate to the US and other countries.

**1842**
The Mines Act bans boys under 10 years and all girls from working underground in mines. Two years later, the Factories Act stops children under 13 from working more than six and a half hours a day.

**1838**
Slavery comes to an end in most of the British Empire. The Slavery Abolition Act had made it illegal to own slaves in most British colonies from 1834, but enslaved people were still forced to work as unpaid 'apprentices' until 1838.

**1853–6**
Britain, France and Turkey fight Russia in the Crimean War. 500,000 people die on the battlefield and of disease. For the first time, photography – a new technology – shows the world what war is like.

# A timeline of slavery

**In the late 18th century, a movement began in Britain to abolish slavery, called the abolitionist movement. Britain had been involved in the transatlantic slave trade since the 16th century. In 1807, it became illegal to buy and sell enslaved people in the British Empire. In 1834, it was made illegal to own slaves too. British slave-owners received money from the government for losing their 'property'. Enslaved people received nothing.**

**1876**
Scotsman Alexander Graham Bell makes the first commercially used telephone.

**1879**
Britain's first electric street lighting is installed in Newcastle.

**1880**
Education is made compulsory for all children under 10. Eleven years later, it becomes free too.

**1859**
Charles Darwin publishes his famous book on evolution, *On the Origin of Species*.

**1857–8**
In British-controlled India, Indian troops rebel against their British commanders in an uprising known in Britain as the Indian Rebellion.

**1901**
Victoria dies, aged 81. Her son becomes King Edward VII.

**1899–1902**
The South African War breaks out between Britain and Dutch settlers, as Britain tries to expand its colonies in Southern Africa.

# ALL CHANGE!

The Industrial Revolution in Britain took place between around 1750 and 1900. The invention of new steam-powered machines meant that goods which were previously made by hand could now be mass-produced in factories. Up and down Britain, tens of thousands of machines spun and weaved cotton. Huge furnaces made iron and steel, which were shaped into railway tracks, boilers, bridges, ships and more. The engines that powered these machines ran on coal from mines in Wales, Scotland and the north of England.

Visit Crystal Palace with our character Will on pages 46–47.

## Workshop of the world

Britain exported its manufactured goods all over the globe, dominating world trade. At one point, it was producing more than half of the world's cotton, iron and coal! Britain made so many of the world's manufactured goods that it became known as the 'workshop of the world'.

In 1851, a Great Exhibition was held to celebrate Britain's industrial achievements. A spectacular exhibition hall called Crystal Palace was built in London to house 100,000 exhibits from Britain and around the world. Over 6 million people – a third of the country's entire population! – visited to gawp at the latest jaw-dropping machinery, inventions, arts and crafts.

## Inventions

**Here are just some of the things that were invented in and around the time of the Victorians. Can you imagine life without them?**

- **Sewing machine (1790)**
- **Steam-powered locomotive (train) (1804)**
- **Photography (1820s)**
- **Telegraph (1830s)**
- **Can opener (1855)**
- **Bicycle with pedals (1860s)**
- **Electric streetlamps and light bulbs (1870s)**
- **Record player (1877)**
- **Telephone (1879)**
- **Motor car (1885)**
- **Moving film (movies) (1895)**
- **X-rays (1895)**
- **Vacuum cleaner (1901)**
- **Aeroplane (1903)**

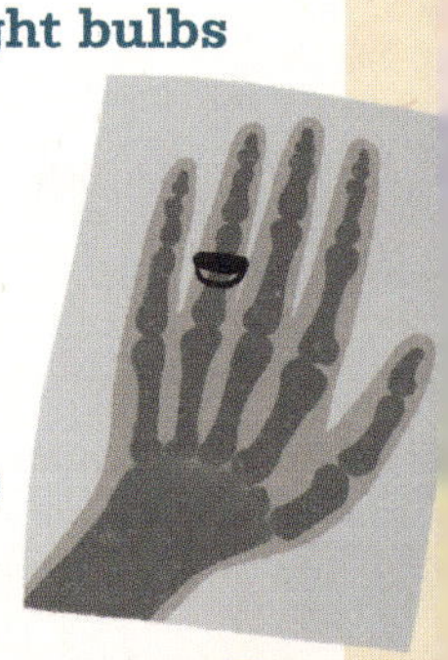

# New ways to travel

The world's first-ever railway journey took place in Wales in 1804. By 1850, about 6,000 miles (almost 10,000km) of track crisscrossed Britain. Railways helped to transform the country. Journey times were slashed from weeks to days. Goods could now be moved quickly from factories to shops all around the country, or to the docks to be shipped abroad. Food from farms could reach towns quicker, making it cheaper. People could live in the suburbs and catch the train to work, or even go on holiday to the seaside.

**The invention of the bicycle gave people more freedom of movement than before.**

**In the early days of the railways, first- and second-class carriages had roofs to protect passengers from the weather.**

**Third-class carriages were open!**

## Railway time

**Before the railways, towns in Britain kept their own time. You can imagine the havoc this caused for train timetables and passengers, as trains set off in one local time zone and arrived in another! The confusion eventually led to the whole country adopting one standard time: London time.**

While the wealthy used horse-drawn carriages and, later, the motor car, to get around, the poor often had to walk.

# VICTORIAN SOCIETY

**Victorian Britain was one of the most powerful nations in the world, but not everyone shared in its wealth. Society was extremely unequal, and life was very different for those who had money and those who did not. Women did not have the same rights and opportunities as men either (see opposite).**

**Upper classes**

## Social class

Victorian society was divided into three main groups: upper class, middle class and working class.

**Upper classes:** Only a small number of people were upper class. Rich upper-class men held most positions of power in government. Their money came from land, property or investments, and they passed their titles and wealth onto their children. Upper-class women and children did not work.

**Middle classes**

**Middle classes:** Industrialization in Britain created a wealthy middle class. By the end of the Victorian period, this group made up over a quarter of the population. Middle-class men had well-paid jobs, working as bankers, lawyers, factory owners, doctors, merchants and engineers. Women and children didn't work.

**Working classes:** Most of the population were working class. Usually men, women and children all worked, often for very little money. They worked as factory workers, servants, labourers, seamstresses, street sellers and more. Skilled manual workers, such as engineers and mechanics, were a little better off.

**Working classes**

## One voice, one vote

In Britain today, everyone over the age of 18 can vote. But when Victoria became queen, only wealthy men who owned property had this right. During her reign, the right to vote was expanded. By 1884, over half of all men could vote. It would take until 1918, though, for the vote to be given to all men over 21 years old.

Some women started to campaign for the right to vote in the mid-1800s, and by the end of the century there was growing support. In 1897, different groups of women united into one group, called the National Union of Women's Suffrage Societies (NUWSS). Some women finally gained the right to vote in 1918.

## What the Dickens?

**Charles Dickens, a famous Victorian writer, felt strongly about the terrible hardships faced by the poor. His novels often drew attention to social issues such as child labour, poverty, crime and factory working conditions. One of his best-known books is *Oliver Twist* (1838), a story about the struggles of a poor orphan boy who runs away from a workhouse (see page 13) and joins a gang of pickpockets.**

## Women's rights

Most Victorians thought it was the man's job to work and provide for his family, while the woman stayed at home. (Of course, in poor families, women had to look after the home *and* go to work.) Women were not allowed to vote and up until 1882, any property a married woman owned belonged to her husband.

**Religion was very important to the Victorians, and many people went to church regularly.**

# WORKING LIVES

**Can you imagine working twelve or more hours a day, six days a week, in a factory or mine, and earning barely enough money to eat? This was the life of many men, women and children in Victorian Britain. Fortunately, working conditions slowly got better through the 19th century.**

## Tough times

In the first half of the Victorian period, the lives of workers were extremely tough. Hours were long, wages were low and the work was often backbreaking and dangerous. Many workplaces were full of hazards, such as open fires and fast-moving machinery. Burns and other accidents were common, and people's lungs were damaged through breathing in dust and smoke. There were no state benefits or pensions for those who were too ill or old to work.

Around a quarter of all workers were children. Many families relied on the money they brought in. You can see some of the jobs that children did on pages 14–15.

In 1889, in London, there was a strike by tailors and tailoresses.

## Making things better

From the 1850s, working conditions began to improve, and more help was offered to those in need:

**Government reform acts:** The government passed laws to improve safety and air quality, and to reduce the working hours of children (see page 15) and women.

**People power:** Workers formed trade unions and some went on strike to improve their working conditions. In the 1870s, many companies agreed to cut the working day from 12 hours to 10 hours, and gave workers Saturday afternoons off.

**Charity:** Philanthropists and the church set up charities for the poor, such as orphanages and soup kitchens, and campaigned for changes in the law.

# Life in the workhouse

People who couldn't support themselves might end up in the workhouse. Here they would be expected to work in return for basic food, clothes, shelter and medical care. Workhouses were grim places. Husbands and wives, sisters and brothers, parents and children were all separated – only children under 7 years old got to stay with their mothers. Here is what a typical day might have been like:

**6am:**

Wake up. A bell rings to wake everyone up. Everyone gets dressed in their uniform.

**6.30am:**

Breakfast. This is usually porridge or thin vegetable soup.

**7am – 6pm:**

Time for work. Jobs include doing the laundry, breaking up stones into rubble, gardening, chopping wood and 'oakum picking' (picking apart the strands of old ropes). At noon there's a break for dinner – stew with bread.

**6pm:**

Work ends. Supper is bread and cheese.

**7pm:**

Free time. There is just one free hour a day.

**8pm:**

Bedtime. People sleep crammed side by side in a big room. Children often shared beds.

# JOBS FOR CHILDREN

Many Victorian children worked. Poor families often had no choice but to send their children out to earn money. Some children only worked part-time and went to school as well. But by the time they were teenagers, most working-class children were working full-time.

## Mine worker

At the start of the Victorian period, many children worked underground in coal mines. The youngest children, aged 3 and up, operated the doors that kept air flowing though the mine, and had to sit alone in the dark for up to 12 hours. Older children hauled heavy carts along the narrow tunnels.

## Mill worker

Cotton mills employed a lot of children because they were cheap. Mills were hot, noisy places, full of dangerous whirring machinery. Accidents were common, and many children became ill from the cotton dust that clogged the air.

## Bird scarer

Children as young as 6 were put to work as bird scarers on farms, frightening off birds to stop them eating the crops. They stood all alone in a field from dawn till dusk, whatever the weather.

## Street seller

Many poor children made a bit of money by selling goods, such as flowers, watercress or fruit, to passers-by on the street.

## Pure finder

Pure finders scoured the streets looking for dog poo (known as 'pure'), which they collected in a big bucket. They sold the poo to tanners, who used it in the leather-making process.

## Mudlark

Mudlarks scavenged the muddy banks of the River Thames and sold anything of value they found – bits of coal, old rope or nails. The job involved wading for hours in stinky mud.

**Some children turned to crime to survive, and became pickpockets.**

## Climbing boy

Boys as young as 4 or 5 worked as climbing boys, clambering up narrow chimneys to sweep them clean. The job was very dangerous – boys suffered burns and sometimes got stuck and died. Climbing boys were banned in 1875.

## Child worker reforms

**The laws listed below were put in place to limit children's working hours. Not everyone obeyed them, but things did slowly improve.**

- **1833: children under 9 banned from working in most factories and mills.**
- **1842: boys under 10 and girls banned from working in coal mines.**
- **1844: in factories, children aged 9–12 are only allowed to work a maximum of six and a half hours a day; 13–18-year-olds can work twelve hours.**
- **1891: no children under 11 are allowed to work in factories.**

# 24 HOURS AS A VICTORIAN BOY

This is what might have happened to our working-class boy, Will, on a typical day in the middle of the 19th century. Will's daily life is hard, but he's luckier than some – the family has enough to eat, and Will spends some of his day at school rather than at work.

## 5.30am: Wake up

At dawn, Will is woken by a tapping at the window. It's the knocker-upper, whose job is to get people up in time for work. Clocks and watches are expensive, so most working-class families don't own one.

## 5.40am: Washing and dressing

Will washes in the bedroom he shares with his family. He uses a bowl of cold water and a flannel – hot water is a once-a-week treat. Afterwards, he pays a visit to the outside toilet. He has to wait a while, because it is shared with people in other houses.

## 6.15am: Off to work

After a cup of tea and some bread, Will and his younger sister walk to work. They both have jobs at the textile mill.

## 7am: Work starts

The working day begins. Will is in the weaving shed, where the machinery is so loud it makes his ears ring. His sister works in the spinning mill next door. She has a terrible, permanent cough.

## Noon: Dinner break

Will has a short break to eat the bread he's brought from home. The boy sitting next to him has red eyes from crying – he's just been beaten after the overseer caught him sleeping.

## 2pm: Off to school

Will's shift ends, but his day isn't over yet – school is about to begin! In the classroom, he can't help yawning as he recites his times tables.

## 5pm: Home time

Finally it's time to go home. Back at the house, Will's mother is fussing over Will's father. He works at the iron foundry and has a new, painful-looking burn on his arm.

## 6pm: Supper

Will is starving! He tucks into soup, potatoes and a small bit of bacon, washed down with tea. Afterwards there's a treat, a boiled pudding with custard. Will's father is fed first – it's important he stays fit and healthy so he can keep earning money.

## 7.30pm: Time for play

It's still light outside, so Will has time to hang out on the street with his friends. They play leapfrog, and then start a game of football using a ball made from old rags.

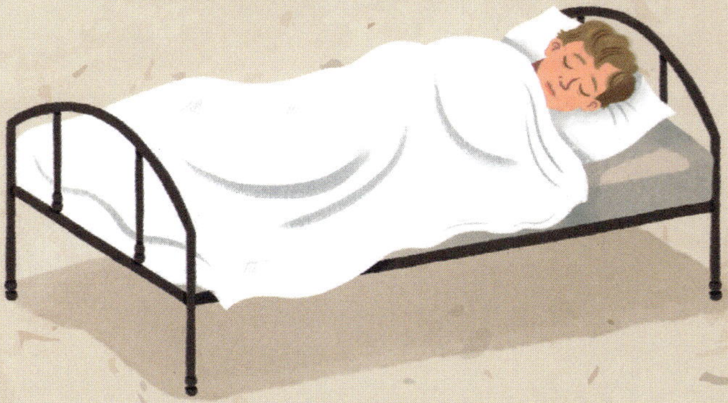

## 9pm: Bedtime

Once it starts getting dark it's time for bed. Will says his prayers in the cold bedroom, and then tumbles into bed and is asleep within seconds.

# VICTORIAN TOWNS

When Queen Victoria was born in 1819, three-quarters of the population lived in the countryside, but by 1901 this had dropped to under a quarter. Towns and cities grew quickly, as millions of people moved away from the countryside to work in factories for better wages.

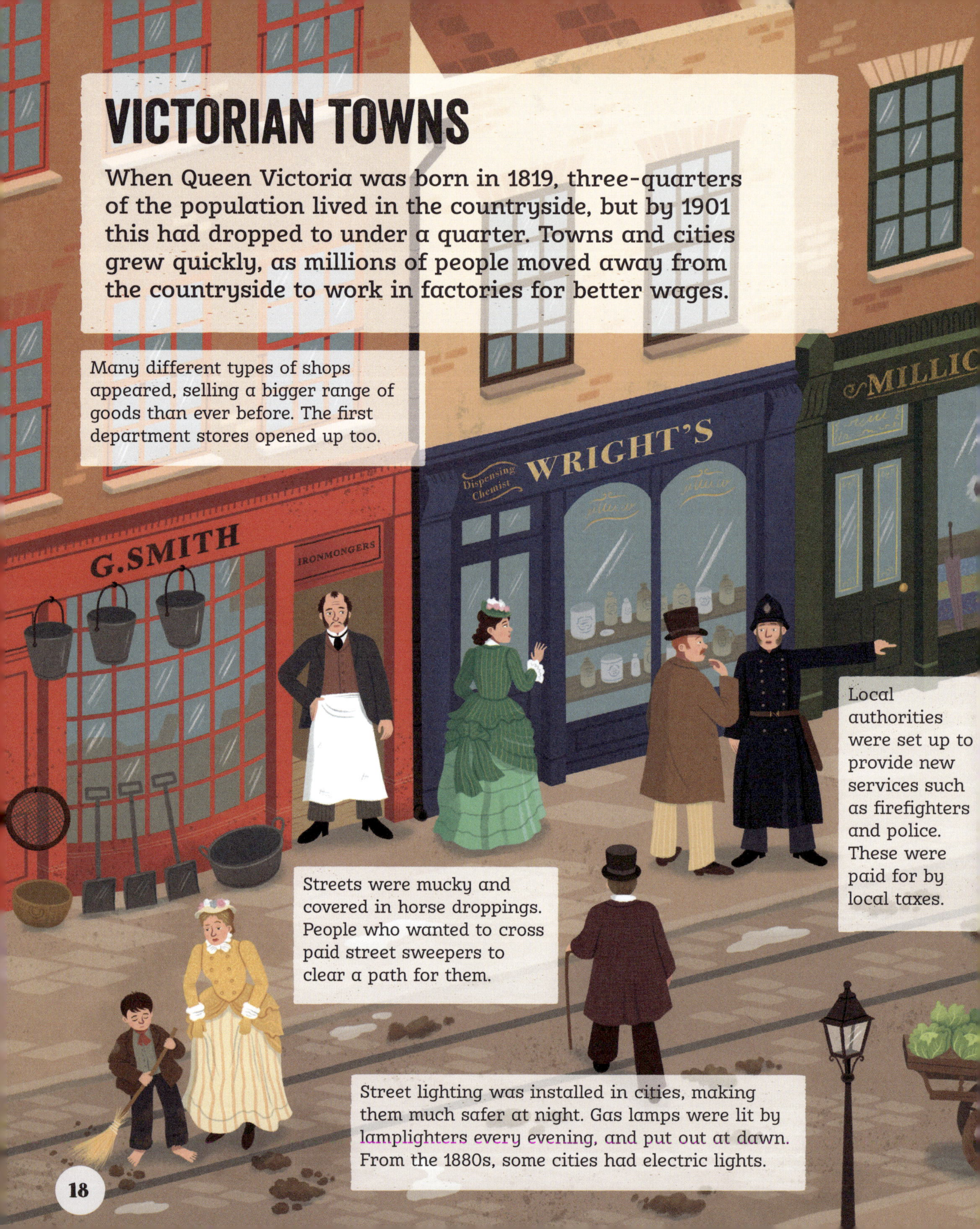


Many different types of shops appeared, selling a bigger range of goods than ever before. The first department stores opened up too.

Local authorities were set up to provide new services such as firefighters and police. These were paid for by local taxes.

Streets were mucky and covered in horse droppings. People who wanted to cross paid street sweepers to clear a path for them.

Street lighting was installed in cities, making them much safer at night. Gas lamps were lit by lamplighters every evening, and put out at dawn. From the 1880s, some cities had electric lights.

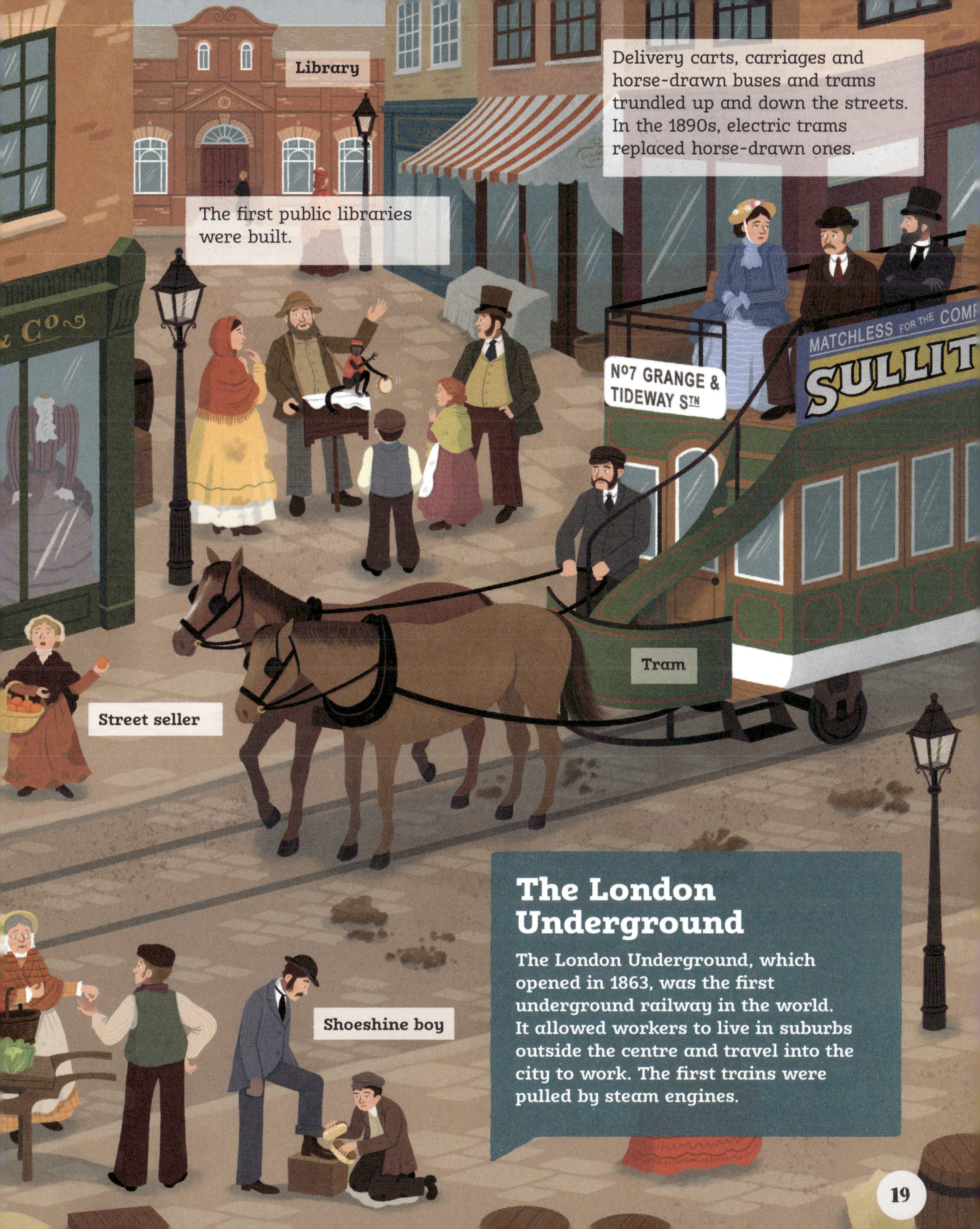


Delivery carts, carriages and horse-drawn buses and trams trundled up and down the streets. In the 1890s, electric trams replaced horse-drawn ones.

The first public libraries were built.

## The London Underground

The London Underground, which opened in 1863, was the first underground railway in the world. It allowed workers to live in suburbs outside the centre and travel into the city to work. The first trains were pulled by steam engines.

# HOMES FOR THE POOR

**The homes of many working class people were grim, especially in cities. Lots of people lived in overcrowded, run-down slums near the factories where they worked. Often, two or more families were crammed into one small house. Sanitation was terrible, which meant outbreaks of disease were common.**

In the early Victorian period, there was no rubbish collection, no proper sewer system and often no clean running water. People had to collect water from pumps in the street, wells, rivers or streams. The water was sometimes contaminated with sewage, which made people ill.

Houses were often cold, damp and mouldy. Temperatures inside and outside were not all that different! Some houses had leaky roofs and broken windows. Landlords were supposed to look after and repair the buildings they owned, but often they didn't bother.

Most people shared a house with another family. It was not unusual for a big family, with perhaps four or five children, to all live, eat and sleep in a single room. Children played out on the streets, because there was no room indoors.

Women who didn't go out to work sometimes made a bit of money by doing jobs from home, like washing other people's laundry or making matchboxes at the kitchen table for up to 12 hours a day. Clothes were hand-washed and put through a machine called a mangle which squeezed the water out so the clothes would dry more quickly.

## Making things better

**In 1848 and 1875 the government passed Public Health Acts. Over time, living conditions in some places began to improve. Better housing and new sewer systems were built and streets were cleaned up. But many people continued to live in terrible conditions.**

**Dozens of houses might share a couple of toilets. Just imagine how filthy they must have got!**

## Model villages

Some factory owners were so concerned about the living conditions in the slums that they moved their factories to the countryside and built new 'model villages' for their workers to live in. Cotton mill owner Titus Salt founded the village of Saltaire in Yorkshire, while the village of Bournville was built by the Cadbury family, close to their chocolate factory outside Birmingham.

Statue of Titus Salt

# HOMES FOR THE WELL-OFF

Well-off Victorians could afford comfortable houses with gardens and lots of space. The growth of railways and other forms of public transport made it possible for middle-class families to live in suburbs on the outskirts of cities and commute to work. These leafy neighbourhoods were a world away from the grime, noise and squalor of the city.

Rooms were lit by oil or gas lamps. Later in the Victorian period, electric lighting began to appear, although only the very rich could afford it in their homes – a single light bulb cost a week's average wages!

Houses might have several bedrooms, rooms in the attic for servants, a kitchen, a separate dining room and a large drawing room, where the family would entertain guests. Most drawing rooms had a piano, which the ladies of the house would play. Houses had running water and, by the end of the Victorian period, flushing toilets and bathrooms with plumbed-in baths. Before this, bathtubs had to be filled up by hand using jugs of hot water.

## Life as a Victorian housemaid

**Most middle-class and upper-class families had one or more servants, who lived in the house and did all the cleaning, cooking and other jobs. With no washing machines or vacuum cleaners, everything had to be done by hand. Maids worked for up to eighteen hours a day, with just half a day off a week.**

**Some households employed just one maid, who would be expected to do everything! In a typical day, she might:**

- **clean out all the fireplaces and re-lay the fires**
- **carry heavy jugs of hot water to fill washstands and baths**
- **help the mistress and children dress**
- **empty the chamberpots**
- **make the beds**
- **sweep, dust and scrub the house**
- **cook the meals and wash up**
- **run errands to the shops**
- **do the laundry (a big job, probably done with extra help)**

Rooms were decorated in the latest styles, with patterned wallpaper, plush rugs and carpets, heavy curtains, paintings and lots of ornaments.

# 24 HOURS AS A VICTORIAN GIRL

This is what might have happened to Dora, our girl from a wealthy middle-class family, on a typical day in the 1870s. Girls like Dora were often brought up by nurses and governesses. In the upper and middle classes, parents didn't always spend much time with their children.

## 7am: Wake up

Dora is woken up by a nursemaid, who helps her wash and get dressed.

## 8am: Breakfast

Breakfast is hot cocoa, a boiled egg and bread with jam. Dora and her siblings eat in the nursery.

## 9am: Lessons

Dora spends the morning doing lessons with her governess – sewing, reading, writing and arithmetic. Next year, when she turns ten, she will start at the local girl's day school, which she'll attend for two or three years. After that, she will stay at home until she gets married.

## 12.30: Lunch

Dora's mother joins the children for lunch. They eat boiled ham and potatoes, followed by a jam roly-poly pudding.

## 1.30pm: Walk in the park

Dora's governess takes the children for a stroll in the park. A man whizzes past on a bicycle, almost knocking Dora off her feet. Her governess tuts – these new-fangled machines are a menace!

## 3pm: To the library

On the way home, they visit the public library. Dora borrows one of her favourite books, *Alice's Adventures in Wonderland*.

## 5pm: Teatime

The nursemaid lays the table for tea. Dora's younger brother is running around and bumps into it, sending everything crashing to the floor. When Dora's mother is told by the nursemaid, she is not happy! She sends him straight to bed without any supper as punishment.

## 6.30pm: Family time

Dora's father is home from work. The children gather in the drawing room to spend some time with their parents. They play a card game called 'Happy Families' and then Dora's father reads aloud to them. The story, by a writer called Anna Sewell, is about a horse called Black Beauty.

## 8pm: Bedtime

Dora says good night to her parents, and the nursemaid takes her up to bed.

### Scrapbooking

**Keeping a scrapbook was a popular hobby for children and women in Victorian times. Scrapbooks could contain all sorts of things, from 'scraps' (small paper images of animals, flowers and other things) to greetings cards, mementoes, poems, pressed flowers and quotes from favourite authors.**

# MAKE PAPER FLOWERS

Well-off Victorian women had plenty of time on their hands, and creating hand-made crafts from paper, beads, feathers, wax and other materials was a common hobby. Making beautiful paper flowers to decorate the home was especially popular. Have a go creating your own bouquet of roses.

## You will need (to make 3 flowers):

- **3 sheets of A4 or US letter paper (in colours of your choice. Each sheet makes one flower)**
- **Compass and scissors**
- **PVA glue**
- **Florist wire, 3 × 12in (30cm) lengths**
- **1 sheet green tissue paper**
- **1 sheet A4 or US letter green paper**
- **Thumbnail-size ball of sticky tack**

**1** Use a compass to draw four circles around 4in (10cm) in diameter on one of the sheets of coloured paper. Cut them out.

**2** Fold each circle in half three times. Then cut around the top corners of each shape, as shown, to make a rounded petal shape. Snip off the bottom tip of the petal. Unfold the circles.

**3** You'll see that each circle is divided into eight 'petals'. Cut out one of the petals from the first circle; cut two petals from the second circle; cut three petals from the third circle; and cut four petals from the fourth circle. Then, from the leftover petals, set aside the three-petal shape and the two-petal shape.

**4** You now have six pieces of paper which will form the six layers of your flower. Take the largest layer and cut halfway along each of the fold lines to separate the petals; then glue together the two outside petals to form a cone shape. Repeat for the other five layers (the smallest layer can just be rolled into a cone).

**5** Cut a strip of green tissue paper slightly larger than the length of florist wire. Wrap this around the wire, using glue to stick it in place. Leave to dry.

**6** On the green paper, draw a circle about 2in (5cm) in diameter. Draw a five-pointed star inside the circle. Use the picture on the right as a guide – it doesn't matter if it's not perfect. Cut it out.

**7** Once the wire is dry, poke it through the centre of the green star and the centre of the largest flower layer, then place a small blob of sticky tack onto the top of the wire, inside the flower. Glue the centre of the green star to the bottom of the flower.

**8** Put a blob of glue on top of the sticky tack, then stick down the second-biggest flower layer on top, inside the other layer. Keep adding blobs of glue and flower layers, one inside another, to create the finished rose. Leave to dry.

**9** Repeat the steps to create two more flowers.

## The language of flowers

**Flowers had important meanings in Victorian times, and people often sent flowers to express their emotions. Each flower had a different meaning, like a secret code. The language of flowers is known as 'floriography'.**

**Rose: love**

**Sweet pea: gratitude**

**Daisy: innocence**

**Rosemary: remembrance**

**Rhododendron: danger**

**Zinnia: friendship**

**Peonies: shyness**

**Yellow carnation: rejection, disdain**

# AT SCHOOL

**When Victoria came to the throne, few children went to school and most people in the country grew up not being able to read or write. But by the end of her reign, all children had to attend school by law, and education was free for everyone, rich and poor, both boys and girls.**

## Education for the wealthy

In well-off families, young children were taught at home by a governess. When boys turned 10, they were sent away to boarding school. There were some schools for girls, but many girls continued to be taught at home. While their brothers studied Greek and Latin, they learnt how to play the piano, sew and run a household.

## Education for the poor

In the early Victorian Age, most working class children had to work to earn money for their families. There were some free schools set up by charities or the church, as well as 'dame schools' run by working-class women in their homes. But most children went to school only occasionally or not at all.

Over time, things began to change. In 1844, a law was passed that children working in factories must be given six half-days of school a week. By 1880, school became compulsory for all 5- to 10-year-olds (later raised to 13). More schools were set up across the country and, in 1891, school fees were abolished.

Victorian schools were very strict. Children were beaten for misbehaving. If they worked too slowly or made a mistake, they might be made to stand on a stool wearing a 'dunce's cap'.

Paper was expensive, so children wrote on slates. Children copied lessons from the blackboard and chanted times tables out loud until they were memorized.

The school day began at 9am and ended at 5pm.

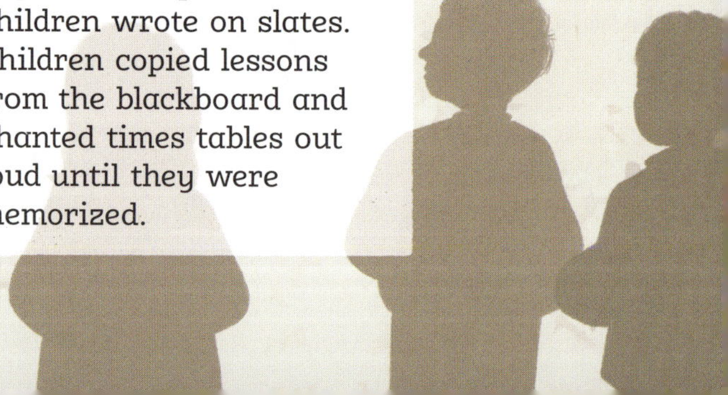

Victorian PE was called 'drill'. It involved simple exercises, such as marching on the spot or swinging arms, performed together in time.

At the end of the school year, children had to pass an exam to move up to the next year. Most children left school when they were 10–12 years old.

Classes could be big – as many as 70 or 80 children. Sometimes older children helped teach the younger ones.

Children were taught reading, writing and arithmetic (known as 'the three Rs'), as well as practical skills such as woodwork for boys and sewing for girls. Later, history and geography were added to the curriculum.

# FASHION

Fashions changed every few decades in the Victorian Age, as styles went in and out of fashion. Clothes were a way to show off social position and wealth. Grand dresses, fine fabrics and fancy frills were a sign that a person didn't need to work for a living.

### Outfit for a woman (1840s)

## Clothes for the rich ... and the poor

Wealthy Victorians changed their clothes several times a day. A rich woman might have day dresses, evening gowns, more relaxed 'tea dresses' for wearing at home, carriage dresses for wearing on carriage rides, horse-riding outfits ... and more!

Many working people owned just one or two sets of clothes, which were bought second-hand or given to them. Things began to change in the mid-1800s when the first practical, easy-to-use sewing machines were developed. This allowed clothes to be made much more quickly and cheaply – it was the start of mass-market, ready-to-wear fashion. By the late Victorian period, many working people could afford to buy brand-new clothes.

The very poorest people in society wore whatever clothes or rags they could get their hands on.

### Super-size skirts

**In the 1850s, women began wearing metal-hooped cages called crinolines, and skirts became enormous. Some were over 15ft (5m) wide!**

### Outfit for a man (1870s)

### Outfit for a woman (1880s)

## A tight squeeze!

**Victorian women of all classes and ages wore stiff undergarments called corsets. These could be tightened to create a tiny waist – something that was very fashionable at the time. The average woman's waist was 22in (56cm), and some were much smaller. Some women ended up with deformed ribs and spines through wearing extremely tight corsets when they were children.**

# HEALTH AND MEDICINE

**There were lots of things that could kill you or make you very sick in Victorian Britain, especially if you were poor. But healthcare and medicine improved dramatically throughout the century, thanks to new discoveries and inventions.**

## Deadly diseases

At the beginning of the Victorian Age, doctors did not know much about the causes of illness, and so were not very good at treating it. Terrible outbreaks of diseases such as cholera, typhoid and tuberculosis regularly swept the country, killing thousands.

Some people thought that cholera was caused by bad air or even by 'cold fruits' like cucumbers and melons. But in the 1850s, a doctor called John Snow worked out that an outbreak in London was caused by people drinking dirty water from a public water pump. The water had been infected by waste leaking from a nearby cesspit.

Soon afterwards, scientists discovered that certain diseases were caused by germs – tiny living things – invading the body. It became clearer that better hygiene would save lives. In 1875, the government passed a Public Health Act that forced local councils to build sewers, collect rubbish and provide a clean water supply.

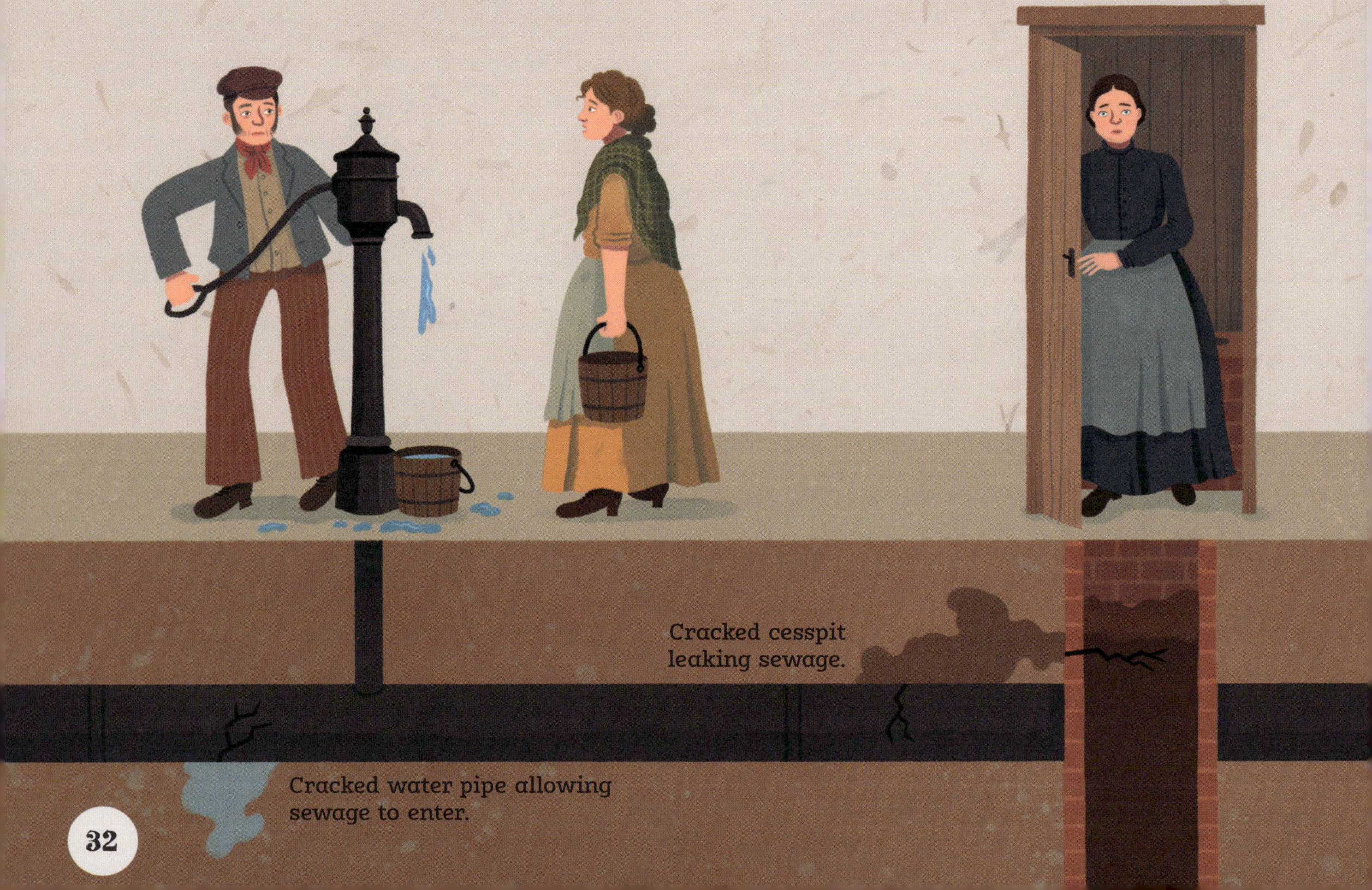

## Antiseptics

In early Victorian hospitals, half of all patients died after surgery. British surgeon Joseph Lister realized this was because their wounds had become infected. At the time, surgeons didn't wash their hands and wore the same bloodstained clothes from one operation to the next. In 1870, Lister began using chemicals, called antiseptics, to clean wounds and surgical instruments, killing the germs. Many more people survived.

Other medical innovations in the Victorian Age included anaesthesia, the stethoscope and X-rays.

## Hospitals and nursing

Florence Nightingale helped to make Victorian hospitals cleaner and turned nursing into a skilled profession. In 1854, she led a team of nurses to the Crimea to care for soldiers injured in the Crimean War. Horrified by the filthy hospital, she had it cleaned from top to bottom and insisted people wash their hands, saving many lives. Later, back in London, she set up the world's first nursing school.

## Hunger and malnutrition

Can you imagine feeling constantly hungry and eating nothing but bread, day after day? This was what life was like for some poor families. Malnutrition led to diseases such as scurvy and rickets, and some people even died of starvation.

As living standards gradually improved, more and more people could afford to eat regularly and healthily. But even at the end of the Victorian period, some people still went hungry.

# LAW AND ORDER

The Victorians were very worried about crime and believed in tough punishments. They thought this would make criminals reflect on what they had done and decide not to break the law again.

## Crime and punishment

When Victoria came to the throne, two of the most common sentences for criminals were execution and transportation to Australia. Children were punished in the same way as adults.

But the Victorians had different ideas about how to deal with crime. They built lots more prisons, and for the first time, made prison the main form of punishment. Their aim was not only to punish criminals, but to try to reform them so that they would lead honest lives in the future. In 1854, special institutions called Reformatory Schools were set up for children.

## On the beat

Before the Victorian Age, it was the job of local communities to catch criminals and keep the streets safe. But in 1829, a politician called Robert Peel set up England's first professional police force, in London. Other parts of the country soon followed. The policemen patrolled a certain area (known as their 'beat') and carried wooden truncheons and rattles in case they needed to call for help.

### Do hard labour like a Victorian prisoner

**Victorian prison work sometimes included pointless tasks such as turning a crank or climbing a treadmill (see opposite), as well as picking oakum (see page 13). Pick one of the tasks below, and see how long it takes before you get tired or bored. Remember, no talking!**

- **Instead of climbing the treadmill, walk up and down stairs.**
- **Instead of picking oakum, take a ball of wool and pull apart the yarn into separate strands.**
- **Instead of turning a crank, draw a big circle on a piece of paper, over and over again.**

# Life behind bars

Victorian prisons were terrible places. Prisoners were not allowed to talk to each other, and were forced to do hard, repetitive work. If they spoke, they were whipped. The authorities hoped that hard work, silence and boredom would make prisoners think about their crimes and decide to be better people. By the end of the Victorian period, it was clear that harsh punishments in prisons did not reduce crime. The treadmill and other cruel practices were abandoned.

Some prisoners were made to turn a crank (a handle) 20 times a minute, up to 10,000 times a day.

The treadmill was a giant circular wheel. Prisoners climbed up the wheel to make it turn, for five or more hours a day. Every ten or fifteen minutes they had a five-minute rest.

# ENTERTAINMENT

**During the second half of Victoria's reign, wages rose and working hours reduced. In 1871, the Bank Holidays Act gave everyone four whole days off work a year. More and more people had the time and money to enjoy leisure activities and new kinds of entertainment.**

## Seaside holidays

The growth of the railways made travel easier and cheaper. For the first time, the middle classes could afford to take short holidays at the seaside. Over time, working-class people began to join them there on day-trips. People paddled in the sea, strolled along promenades and pleasure piers, ate 'penny lick' ice creams, rode donkeys along the sand and watched Punch and Judy shows.

By the 1880s, some rich Victorians were even travelling abroad for their holidays, to Europe and Egypt. The first travel agent was a businessman called Thomas Cook. He began running trips to the seaside in 1841.

## Public parks

Free public parks opened in many towns and cities, with flower displays, paths for promenading and bandstands where brass bands played on summer evenings and Sundays. These green spaces were open to everyone, rich and poor.

## Music, theatre and art

In cities, people visited new museums and art galleries and listened to public lectures on science and other topics. The invention of electric lighting allowed theatres and concert halls to stay open late into the evening. Rich people dressed up in their finest clothes to go to the opera and theatre, while for the working classes there were cheaper music halls, which put on variety shows – a mix of music, comedy and plays.

Magic lantern shows were very popular. Painted images or photographs were projected onto screens or walls, accompanied by music, sound effects and storytelling. Then, in the 1890s, the first, very short, silent moving pictures were shown in London – cinema had arrived!

## Books for all

As books got cheaper and people became better educated, greater numbers of people could enjoy reading. After 1850, free public libraries opened in many towns and cities.

Some authors, including Charles Dickens, published their novels in monthly instalments. This meant more people could afford them, and also kept readers in suspense from month to month. For children, there were exciting books such as *Treasure Island*, *The Jungle Book* and *Alice's Adventures in Wonderland*.

**In well-off homes, groups of people liked to entertain themselves by playing parlour games, such as charades.**

# DORA GOES TO THE SEASIDE

Today is the first day of my family's seaside holiday! We are staying in a smart hotel on the seafront, and from my window I can see the sea sparkling beneath a perfect, blue sky. On the beach, bathing machines on wheels are being pulled up and down the pebbles, and I can just about make out tiny figures splashing in the waves. My mother is going to take a dip in the sea today and she has promised me and my sister that if we are well-behaved we can join her!

First, though, she insists we all take a stroll along the seafront promenade. She says the sea air will be good for our health, but I think she just wants a chance to show off her expensive new dress and parasol to as many people as possible. My mother and father set off in front, while the rest of us children follow behind with our governess. I feel hot and sticky in my corset and thick petticoats. In the distance I can see people strolling along the new pleasure pier. What a splendid sight it is!

Just ahead, a noisy crowd has gathered around a Punch and Judy puppet show. My little brother dawdles as we pass, hoping to watch, but our governess hauls him away. My father frowns at the loud bursts of rowdy laughter coming from the crowd – he thinks too many common people come to the seaside nowadays, and says next year we might go abroad. I hope not – I love it here!

When we reach the bandstand, father treats us all to a penny lick ice cream. I lick the shallow glass bowl completely clean as we listen to the brass band play – nothing is more delicious than cold ice cream on a hot day! When my mother spots a photographer's studio over the road, she insists on having a family portrait taken. Inside the studio it's cool and dark. The photographer positions us in front of a backdrop painted to look like a beach, with real pebbles underneath our feet. We all pose very formally, serious and unsmiling, except for my little brother, who pulls a silly face. Mother won't be happy about that when she sees the photo!

After lunch, it's finally time for a dip! Our governess takes my younger brothers to play with their new wooden buckets and spades, while my mother and sister and I climb up into the bathing machine we have hired. Father is swimming in a different part of the beach, just for men. As the hut bumps and jolts its way down to the sea, we change into our bathing costumes – long trousers and tunics – and hang up our hats and dresses.

Once the hut comes to a halt in the shallow water, I fling open the door, clamber down the steps into the sea ... and let out a loud yelp! It's freezing! My mother only gets as far as her ankles before she turns around, laughing. Instead, she sits on the steps in the sunshine, watching me and my sister splashing and jumping in the waves. The seaside is my favourite place in the world!

# MAKE A TOY THEATRE

Toy theatres were very popular in Victorian times. These miniature paper theatres reproduced popular plays of the time and were sold as kits that could be assembled at home. Each kit came with scenery, characters and a shortened script, so that families could reenact the play.

## You will need:

- **Cereal box**
- **Scissors**
- **Acrylic or poster paint**
- **Several sheets of A4 or US letter white card**
- **Sticky tape (optional) and PVA glue**
- **1 sheet tissue paper**
- **12in (30cm) ribbon**
- **Long sticks, such as wooden skewers or straws**

**1** Open out your cereal box. Following the picture to the right, draw a rectangular slot onto the side of the box, just over 1in (3cm) wide. Draw another large rectangle on the front of the box, leaving a border of about 1in (3cm) around the edges.

**2** Measure the side of your box (marked A in the picture). Then measure the same amount in from the edge of the large rectangle (marked B in the picture) and draw a line down the large rectangle as shown.

**3** Cut out the rectangular slot and the shaded area of the large rectangle (see picture). Next, cut along the dashed lines and fold along the dotted line shown in the picture – this rectangle will be folded back later to make the theatre's stage.

**4** Now you are ready to paint your theatre! Use brown or black paint for the stage area. Choose any colour you like for the rest of the theatre. Leave to dry.

**5** Cut a strip of white card long enough to fit along the top of your stage (join together two strips of card if needed). Cut curved shapes along the bottom edge, as shown, and paint it. Leave to dry. To make your stage curtains, cut out two squares of tissue paper, long enough to go from the top of your stage to the bottom. Cut the ribbon in half. Gather a tissue paper square in the centre and tie a ribbon around it, then repeat for the other square. Glue the curtains to either side of the stage. Glue the curved piece of card over the curtains, at the top of the stage.

**6** Draw your characters onto white card and cut them out, then attach them to the ends of the sticks using glue or sticky tape.

**7** Reassemble the box and glue the edges together, leaving one side open. Fold back the theatre stage. Leave to dry. Draw a background scene on a piece of white card, and slip it into the open side of the box. You could draw extra scenes too, to swap in. Your theatre is now ready!

**You can move your characters around the stage from above, by placing the sticks through the narrow rectangular slot.**

1

2

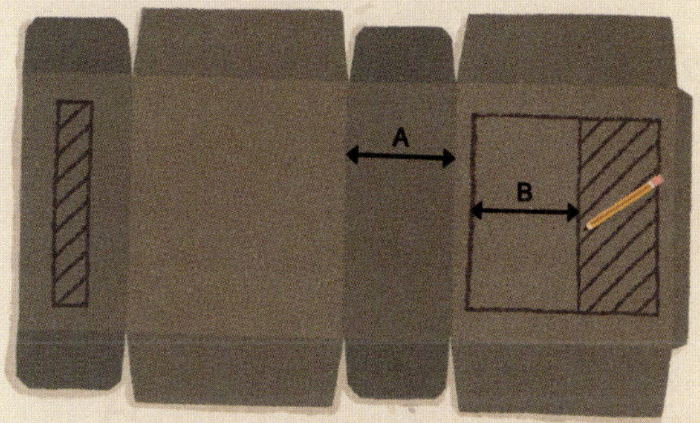


3

4

5

6

7

# SPORTS AND EXERCISE

**Sport was incredibly popular with Victorian men. As well as being good for health, it was thought to encourage values like discipline, teamwork, competitiveness and a sense of fair play. For women, opportunities to play sport were more limited.**

## Cricket

Cricket was extremely popular in Victorian England, and matches drew large crowds. The cricketer W.G. Grace was one of the most famous men in England. The first international cricket match was played in 1877, between England and Australia.

## Football and rugby

Before the 1800s, 'football' was a rough game with no rules. By the 1840s, pupils at two public schools, Rugby and Eton, had developed two slightly different versions of the game: at Rugby, players could pick up the ball, but at Eton, they used only their feet. These two games would go on to become – you guessed it – modern rugby and football. The Football Association was formed in 1863 to agree a proper set of national rules, with the Rugby Football Union following in 1871.

Watching football became incredibly popular from the 1870s. Football teams were set up by workers all around the country – at one point, there were over 800 clubs in Birmingham alone! Teams all over Britain took part in the first FA Cup in 1871, and in 1888 the Football League was formed.

## Lawn tennis

The modern game of tennis was invented in 1873 by a Victorian army officer, who called his version 'sphairistike' and sold sets containing balls, racquets and nets. Four years later, the first men's tennis championship was held in Wimbledon. Lawn tennis became all the rage, played by both men and women.

## Cycling

Cycling became very popular after the 'safety bicycle' appeared in 1884, replacing the precarious penny-farthing and other models. Bicycles became increasingly affordable for ordinary working people, and cycling clubs sprung up around the country. For women, cycling meant ... freedom! Hundreds of thousands of women took up the activity.

## Sports for women

The Victorians frowned on women doing vigorous exercise. They thought it was unladylike, and even dangerous for the delicate female body! Instead, women were encouraged to take part in gentle activities such as walking, dancing and croquet. Later on, things did begin to change, as women began playing lawn tennis and took up cycling. Some women hiked and climbed mountains too.

# AGE OF EMPIRE

When Victoria became queen, Britain already governed some other parts of the world, including areas of Canada, India, Australia and Africa. By the time she died in 1901, Britain's empire had expanded to become the biggest and most powerful in world history. This map shows the British Empire in 1901, when almost a quarter of the world's population lived under British rule.

■ = British Empire

**Canada**

Britain grew wealthy from trade with its empire. Ships arrived in Britain loaded with cotton, rubber and other raw materials from its colonies. They carried away goods made in British factories, such as textiles and machinery, to sell abroad.

Britain had the world's largest navy, and was its leading shipbuilder. By the 1880s, ships powered by sails had been replaced by faster steamships.

**Africa**

Missionaries from Britain travelled to Africa and other parts of the empire to try to spread the Christian religion.

British explorers set off on expeditions into the interior of Africa, which Europeans knew little about. Accounts of their adventures made them famous in Britain. They named Africa's largest lake, Lake Victoria, after the British queen.

# End of the Empire

**In the twentieth century, Britain's empire gradually broke down and countries gained their independence.**

**The British Empire left behind new roads, railways, hospitals, schools and technologies in the countries it colonized. However, it also took away wealth and resources from these places. People living in the colonized countries had British values, customs and laws imposed on them, and were often treated unfairly.**

Britain's East India Company began trading with India in the 17th century and gradually gained more and more control over it. In 1858, the British government began to rule India directly. Queen Victoria called India the 'jewel in the crown' of her empire.

**Suez Canal**

**India**

From the 1850s, British and Irish people were encouraged to emigrate to colonies such as Australia, New Zealand and Canada. Hundreds of thousands left, hoping for a better life.

**Lake Victoria**

The Suez canal in Egypt was completed in 1869, shortening sea journeys to India and the Far East. For years, Britain and France owned the canal together.

**Australia**

From the 1870s, Britain and other European countries began to lay claim to large areas of Africa. In 1884, they divided the continent up between them by drawing lines on a map.

**New Zealand**

# WILL VISITS THE GREAT EXHIBITION

Today I went with my family to visit the Great Exhibition in London. Have you heard about it? It's a big show filled with incredible machines, crafts, inventions and other things from all around the world. It's taken ages to save up for the trip, but Dad says it's worth going without bacon and potatoes for a few months to see the greatest show on Earth! The mill where I work has given everyone a day off work to visit the exhibition, and there are cheap 'shilling day' tickets in the week. We got up really early to catch the train to London. When we finally arrived, hot and uncomfortable, we followed the crowds of excited, chattering people making their way to Hyde Park. I've never seen so many people in one place! And finally, there it was, the famous Crystal Palace exhibition hall – a gigantic building made of glass, glittering in the sunlight.

Once we got inside, my eyes nearly popped out of my head at how big everything was. Gigantic trees towered above our heads and there was a fountain in the middle of the hall that was taller than our house! Mum said there were one hundred thousand exhibits. Can you imagine?

Let me tell you some of the amazing things I saw. There was a machine that printed thousands of newspapers an hour, an electric telegraph that could send messages over long distances (like magic!) and a bed that tipped the sleeper onto the floor at a certain time to wake them up – I'd like one of those. Lots of different countries had displays around the hall. There were sledges and furs from Russia, enormous vases from China, colourful rugs from Turkey, a fire engine from Canada and a stuffed elephant with a big seat on its back that had come all the way from India.

In the middle of the day, we bought pies and tea from the food stalls and paid a penny to visit the toilets, which were so fancy they flushed water when you pulled a handle. After we'd eaten, we joined a big queue to see the Koh-i-Noor diamond. Mum says it's the biggest in the whole world, but I couldn't see what all the fuss was about – it was just a lump of rock. My brother and I were much more excited by the velocipede, a vehicle with four wheels powered by foot pedals. Maybe one day I'll have a go at riding one.

By the end of the day, my feet were aching. Sitting on the train back home, I couldn't stop talking about all the incredible things I'd seen. Tomorrow it's back to work as usual, but I'll never forget the Great Exhibition for as long as I live.

# MAKE CHRISTMAS CRACKERS

**Did you know that many of the Christmas traditions we love today were invented or became popular at the time of the Victorians? One of their creations was the Christmas cracker. Why not make your own Victorian-style crackers for your family or friends?**

## A cracking invention

Crackers were invented by a London sweet maker called Tom Smith around 1847. He began by selling sugared almonds wrapped in twisted paper, with a short love poem inside, but these didn't really catch on. One night, as Tom sat listening to the loud cracks of burning logs on the fire, he thought how fun it would be if his sweets made a surprise 'pop' as they were unwrapped. By the 1860s, his crackers had taken on the shape we recognize today, with a motto and small trinket inside (hats were added later) and a very loud SNAP!

## You will need (to make 4 crackers):

- **8 toilet roll tubes**
- **Crepe paper, around 4ft (1.4m)**
- **Scissors**
- **PVA glue**
- **Old magazines (optional)**
- **Plain paper and pens**
- **4 cracker snaps**
- **Ribbon, around 16ft (5m)**

**1** Cut out four squares of crepe paper, each around 12 × 12in (30 × 30cm). Cut four of the toilet roll tubes in half.

**2** Lay a toilet roll tube along one edge of the crepe paper, with a half-size tube at either end. Make sure there is around 2in (5cm) of space between the tubes. Add glue to the edge of the crepe paper. Then roll up the paper and stick it in place using more glue.

**3** Victorian crackers were decorated with little pictures. You could draw your own small picture, or cut one out from a magazine and stick it onto some paper. Glue the picture onto the side of the cracker.

**4** The first Christmas crackers contained a short love poem known as a motto; in the early 1900s these were replaced by jokes. On a small piece of paper, write a poem or joke to go inside your cracker.

**5** It's time to fill your cracker. Insert the cracker snap, the poem or joke, and a small gift – this could be a sweet or something else. The first Victorian crackers were filled with sweets, but these were soon replaced with small toys and trinkets such as jewellery.

**6** Cut two 24in (60cm) lengths of ribbon and tie them around each end of the cracker in a bow. Your first cracker is complete! Make the other crackers in the same way.

## A Victorian Christmas

**Here are some other Christmas traditions the Victorians introduced:**

**Cards: Christmas cards were invented by the Victorians in the 1840s. By the 1880s, millions were sent every year.**

**Family time: The Victorians made Christmas an important family occasion. People exchanged gifts, played games and ate a big Christmas dinner together.**

**Tree: The tradition of decorating a fir tree came from Germany originally, but Queen Victoria's German husband, Albert, made it popular and fashionable in Britain.**

**Paper chains: These decorations were first seen in the mid-eighteenth century, when they were used to decorate Christmas trees.**

# VICTORIAN FOOD AND RECIPES

There was no such thing as a 'typical' Victorian diet. What people ate depended on when and where they lived, and how much money they had. Some families ate virtually nothing but bread or potatoes, while others tucked into lavish three-course dinners and fancy afternoon teas. Here are a few Victorian recipes you can try out for yourself.

## Mulligatawny soup

Curry-flavoured foods had become very popular in Britain by the mid-nineteenth century. This soup originally came from the Indian subcontinent, but was adapted by the British.

### Ingredients:

- **1 onion**
- **2 sticks celery**
- **1 carrot**
- **1½oz (40g) butter**
- **1 tbsp medium curry powder**
- **2 pints (1 litre) chicken or vegetable stock**
- **3½oz (100g) basmati rice**
- **(optional) cooked chicken, diced**

**1** Finely chop the onion, carrot and celery, then fry with the butter in a large saucepan over a low heat for around 10 minutes until soft, stirring frequently.

**2** Add the curry powder and cook, stirring, for a couple of minutes.

**3** Add the stock, turn up the heat and bring to the boil.

**4** Turn the heat down to a simmer, then add the rice and cook for 15–20 minutes, stirring occasionally. Stir in the cooked chicken, if using, a few minutes before serving.

**Most people shopped for food every day, as there were no fridges to keep it fresh.**

### Improving diets

**Hunger and malnutrition were common at the start of Victoria's reign, but diets improved as wages rose and the price of food fell. By the 1860s, many working-class families could afford to add a small bit of meat to their basic diet of bread or potatoes, as well as some treats like butter, tea and treacle.**

# Treacle tart

The Victorians loved their puddings! Treacle tart and syrup sponge pudding became very popular after golden syrup was invented in the 1880s.

## Ingredients:

- **Sheet of ready-rolled shortcrust pastry**
- **¾ pint (450ml) golden syrup**
- **1¾oz (50g) fresh breadcrumbs**
- **1 lemon, zest and juice**
- **Baking paper**
- **Baking beans**

**1** Preheat the oven to 375°F (190°C/170°C fan).

**2** Line a 8½-in (22-cm) tart tin with the pastry. Lay baking paper over the pastry and weigh it down with baking beans. Bake for 15 minutes, then remove the paper and beans and return to the oven for another 5 minutes until the pastry is golden brown.

**3** For the filling, mix together the golden syrup, breadcrumbs and lemon juice and zest. Pour this into the pastry case and bake for around 30 minutes.

# Workhouse gruel

Gruel was one of the main foods eaten in the workhouse and in prisons. Try this recipe and see if you can manage to finish a whole bowl of it!

## Ingredients:

- **2 tbsp oats**
- **1 pint (500ml) water**
- **Pinch of salt**

**1** Add the oatmeal and water to a pan and boil for 10 minutes.

**2** Add the salt, and leave to cool. Serve lukewarm.

# Lemonade

## Ingredients:

- **3 large lemons, zest and juice**
- **5oz (150g) caster sugar**
- **2 pints (1 litre) water**

**1** Place the ingredients in a large jug. Cover and leave in the fridge for 2 days, stirring occasionally.

**2** Strain the lemonade before drinking.

# COULD YOU LIVE LIKE A VICTORIAN?

**The Victorian era was a time of exciting change and opportunity, but life for ordinary people could be very tough. Do you think you would have liked to live like a Victorian? Think about the questions here and talk about your answers with a friend, parent, carer or teacher.**

**1** The Victorians had a strong sense of what they thought was right and proper behaviour. Look at this list – how much do you agree or disagree with these Victorian values?

- People should work hard
- Honour and fair play is important (no cheating!)
- Men should earn the money while women stay at home
- People should be self-reliant and help themselves
- Children should be well-behaved and respectful (or as the Victorians put it, 'Children should be seen and not heard'!)

**2** Look back at pages 28–29 about Victorian school life. Do you think you would have enjoyed going to school back then? How is the Victorian school day different to yours? Are there any similarities? Is there anything you think the Victorians did better?

**3** 'Object lessons' were common in Victorian classrooms. Teachers would ask children to pick up, observe and study a common object. A silk worm cocoon, for example, might lead to children investigating nature (insect life cycles), geography (the parts of the world where silk worms live) and technology (how silk fabric is manufactured). Do your own object lesson: pick a common object in your house or outside, and find out as much about it as you can.

**4** Many working class people lived in terrible housing. Which of these things do you think you would have found the hardest to cope with?

- No running water – all water for cooking, drinking and washing has to be collected from the standpipe
- Outside toilet, shared with several other families
- Sharing a bedroom with your entire family – no privacy!
- House is cold and damp

**5** There were lots of new types of entertainment in Victorian Britain, from museums and music halls to sports such as tennis, football and cycling. What activities do you think you would have liked to do for fun if you had lived in Victorian times? Are there any activities you enjoy today that you would not have been able to do back then?

**6** Victorian children convicted of committing a crime, such as stealing, might be locked away for months or years. Why do you think children committed these crimes? Do you think the punishment was fair? Which of these aims do you think it achieved?

- Deter others from committing crime
- Punish the offender
- Reform the offender so they won't do it again
- Protect the public

**7** Many Victorian children started work very young. Even when school became compulsory, many children worked part-time or left school for good around the age of 10. How do you think you would have felt about this? What age do you think children should start work? Do you think making children go to school is a good thing?

**8** If you time-travelled back to Victorian times, what three things do you think you would miss the most from your modern-day life? Is there anything you'd like to take from the time of the Victorians and bring back to the modern world?

# Glossary

**anaesthesia**
Medicine given to patients so that they do not feel pain when they are being treated.

**apprentice**
A person who works with someone so that they can learn how to do the job themselves.

**bathing machines**
Changing rooms on wheels that people or horses pulled into the sea. This allowed swimmers to enter the sea without being seen in their bathing costume.

**cesspit**
An underground tank that collects sewage.

**chamber pot**
A bowl kept in the bedroom and used as a toilet at night.

**colonies**
Countries or areas that are under the control of another country (usually far away from it).

**curriculum**
The subjects studied in a school or college.

**emigrate**
To leave a country permanently to go and live in another one.

**empire**
A large area of different lands and peoples, all ruled by one person or government.

**expedition**
A long journey made for a particular reason, for example, to explore another continent.

**evolution**
The process by which living things adapt and change over time. Charles Darwin's theory of evolution explained how life on Earth developed from simple life forms billions of years ago.

**fair play**
Following the rules of a game, showing respect to others and not cheating.

**famine**
An extreme shortage of food affecting large numbers of people.

**foundry**
A factory where metal is melted down and poured into moulds to form different objects.

**governess**
A woman who lives with a family and teaches their children at home.

**hygiene**
The practice of keeping clean to stay healthy.

**malnutrition**
A condition that happens when a person does not eat the right amount of proper food. It can lead to shorter heights, illness and disease.

**missionaries**
People who go to another country to teach their religious beliefs to the people who live there.

**nursemaid**
A servant who lives with a family and helps to care for the children.

**orphanage**
A home for children whose parents are dead or who are unable to look after them.

**philanthropist**
A person who gives money or other help to improve the lives of others.

**pickpocket**
Someone who steals things from people.

**parlour games**
Group games that were played indoors, often in the drawing room. Examples include charades and blind man's buff.

**promenading**
Strolling slowly along a path or promenade for pleasure.

**Punch and Judy**
A traditional puppet show which was very popular in the Victorian era, featuring the characters Mr Punch and his wife Judy.

**reform**
Changing something or someone to make it or them better.

**sanitation**
The process of keeping the public healthy and preventing disease by removing garbage and human waste (wee and poo).

**seamstress**
A person whose job is sewing and making clothes.

**sewer**
A pipe or channel that carries away dirty water and human waste.

**slavery**
The practice of owning other people as property and forcing them to work.

**slum**
A very poor, rundown and crowded area of housing, usually in a city or town.

**soup kitchen**
A place where free food is given to poor and hungry people.

**steamship**
A steam-powered ship. The steam engines turn propellers to move the ship through the water.

**suburb**
An area on the outer edge of a large town or city. People who live in the suburbs often travel to the city for work.

**tanner**
A person who treats animal hides to turn them into leather.

**telegraph**
A way of sending messages over long distances using coded signals. The electric telegraph was invented in the mid-19th century.

**textiles**
Woven or knitted cloth.

**trade union**
A group of workers in a particular trade or industry who join together to bargain for better working conditions or pay.

**tram**
A bus-like vehicle that runs on metal tracks and carries passengers in a town or city.

**transatlantic slave trade**
The name given to the forced enslavement and carrying of people from Africa across the Atlantic Ocean to the Americas.

**transportation**
A form of punishment in which convicted criminals – including children as young as 11 – were sent to faraway British colonies, where they were forced to do hard labour.

# About the author

Claire Saunders has been writing and editing books for more than 20 years. Specializing in children's non-fiction, she has authored or co-authored many titles including *Live Like a Roman*, *Live Like a Viking*, *Live Like an Ancient Egyptian* and *Live Like a Tudor* (for Button Books), *The Power Book*, *The Birthday Almanac*, *A World of Gratitude* and various activity books, including the *Africana Activity Book*, the *National Monuments of the USA Activity Book* and the *Football Fantastic Activity Book*. A graduate of Cambridge University, she has previously worked for Ivy Press and Rough Guides and still loves travelling the world, learning about the history of other cultures. She lives with her family in Lewes, southern England.

**Acknowledgements**

Thanks to Dr Rachel Bright for her expert knowledge and help.

First published 2025 by Button Books, an imprint of Guild of Master Craftsman Publications Ltd, Castle Place, 166 High Street, Lewes, East Sussex, BN7 1XU, UK. www.buttonbooks.co.uk.  ISBN 978 1 78708 182 6. Distributed by Publishers Group West in the United States.  The EEA authorised representative is Authorised Rep Compliance Ltd. Ground Floor, 71 Baggot Street Lower, Dublin, D02 P593, Ireland. www.arccompliance.com. A catalogue record for this book is available from the British Library. Publisher: Jonathan Bailey, Production: Jim Bulley, Senior Project Editor: Susie Behar, Design Manager: Robin Shields, Designer: Ellie Smith, Illustrator: Wesley Robins. Colour origination by GMC Reprographics. Printed and bound in China.

FSC
www.fsc.org
MIX
Paper | Supporting responsible forestry
FSC® C020056

BUTTON BOOKS

**For more on Button Books, contact:**
**GMC Publications Ltd, Castle Place,**
**166 High Street, Lewes, East Sussex,**
**BN7 1XU, United Kingdom**
**Tel: +44 (0)1273 488005**
**buttonbooks.co.uk · buttonbooks.us**

Nº7 GRANGE &
TIDEWAY Sᵀᴺ
MATCHLESS FOR THE COMP
SULLIT
& CO

WRIGHT'S
G.SMITH